March/Marzo

By/Por Robyn Brode

Reading Consultant/Consultora de lectura: Linda Cornwell,
Literacy Connections Consulting/consultora de lectoescritura

WEEKLY READER®
PUBLISHING

Please visit our web site at **www.garethstevens.com**.
For a free catalog describing our list of high-quality books, call 1-800-542-2595 (USA)
or 1-800-387-3178 (Canada). Our fax: 1-877-542-2596

Library of Congress Cataloging-in-Publication Data
    [March. Spanish & English]
    March / by Robyn Brode ; reading consultant, Linda Cornwell — Marzo / por Robyn Brode ;
consultora de lectura, Linda Cornwell.
        p. cm. — (Months of the year — Meses del año)
    Includes bibliographical references and index.
    English and Spanish in parallel text.
    ISBN-10: 1-4339-1931-1   ISBN-13: 978-1-4339-1931-2 (lib. bdg.)
    ISBN-10: 1-4339-2108-1   ISBN-13: 978-1-4339-2108-7 (softcover)
    1. March (Month)—Juvenile literature.   2. Holidays—United States—Juvenile literature.
3. Spring—United States—Juvenile literature.   I. Cornwell, Linda.   II. Title.   III. Title: Marzo.
GT4803.B76918   2010
394.262—dc22   2009013361

This edition first published in 2010 by
Weekly Reader® Books
An Imprint of Gareth Stevens Publishing
1 Reader's Digest Road
Pleasantville, NY 10570-7000 USA

Executive Managing Editor: Lisa M. Herrington
Senior Editors: Barbara Bakowski, Jennifer Magid-Schiller
Designer: Jennifer Ryder-Talbot
Translators: Tatiana Acosta and Guillermo Gutiérrez

Photo Credits: Cover, back cover, title © Masterfile; pp. 11, 13, 21 © Ariel Skelley/Weekly Reader;
p. 7 © Comstock Images; p. 9 © Kameel4u/Shutterstock; p. 15 © Ariel Skelley/Jupiter Images; p. 17
(top left) © Jemal Countess/WireImage/Getty Images; p. 17 (top right) © Evening Standard/Getty
Images; p. 17 (bottom left) © AP Images; p. 17 (bottom right) © Time & Life Pictures/Getty Images;
p. 19 © Getty Images

Printed in the United States of America

1 2 3 4 5 6 7 8 9 10 11 10 09

Table of Contents/Contenido

Boldface words appear in the glossary.
- - - - - - -
Las palabras en **negrita** aparecen en el glosario.

Welcome to March!

March is the third month of the year.

March has 31 days.

- - - - - - - - - -

¡Bienvenidos a marzo!

Marzo es el tercer mes del año.

Marzo tiene 31 días.

Months of the Year/Meses del año

Month/Mes	Number of Days/ Días en el mes
1 January/Enero	31
2 February/Febrero	28 or 29*/28 ó 29*
3 March/Marzo	**31**
4 April/Abril	30
5 May/Mayo	31
6 June/Junio	30
7 July/Julio	31
8 August/Agosto	31
9 September/Septiembre	30
10 October/Octubre	31
11 November/Noviembre	30
12 December/Diciembre	31

*February has an extra day every fourth year./Febrero tiene un día extra cada cuatro años.

In March, winter ends. **Spring** usually begins on March 20.

– – – – – – – – – –

En marzo se acaba el invierno. La **primavera** suele comenzar el 20 de marzo.

Time for Spring

In some places, the weather in March can be cold and windy. Then it can turn warm and sunny.

- - - - - - -

Llega la primavera

En algunos lugares, puede hacer un tiempo frío y ventoso en marzo. Pero el tiempo puede cambiar y volverse soleado y agradable.

What is the weather like in March where you live?

- - - - - - -

¿Que tiempo hace en marzo en el lugar donde vives?

Daylight saving time begins in March. In many places, people turn their clocks forward one hour. Now there will be an extra hour of daylight.

— — — — — — —

En marzo **cambia la hora oficial**. En muchos lugares, se adelantan los relojes una hora. Así se gana una hora más de luz al día.

In March, we plant seeds. We water them and watch the plants grow.

- - - - - -

En marzo, plantamos las semillas. Las regamos y vemos cómo crecen las plantas.

seeds/
semillas

In March, some kids have a spring **vacation** from school. Other kids take a break in April. Then it is time to go back to school.

- - - - - - -

En marzo, algunos niños tienen sus **vacaciones** de primavera. Otros niños las tienen en abril. Después, hay que volver a la escuela.

What do you like to do during your spring vacation?

- - - - - - -

¿Qué te gusta hacer en tus vacaciones de primavera?

14

Special Celebrations

March is Women's History Month. We learn about famous women in history.

- - - - - - -

Celebraciones especiales

En marzo se celebra el Mes de la Historia de la Mujer. Estudiamos la vida de mujeres famosas.

Amelia Earhart
pilot/piloto

Sally Ride
astronaut/astronauta

Maya Angelou
writer/escritora

Michelle Obama
First Lady/Primera Dama

March 17 is **Saint Patrick's Day**. It is an Irish holiday. Some people celebrate by wearing green clothes.

— — — — — — —

El 17 de marzo es el **Día de San Patricio**, una fiesta irlandesa. Para celebrarlo, algunas personas se visten de verde.

When March ends, it is time for April to begin. In some places, April brings rain. Flowers start to **bloom**.

– – – – – – –

Cuando marzo termina, empieza abril. En algunos lugares, con abril llegan las lluvias. Las plantas empiezan a **florecer**.

Glossary/Glosario

bloom: to blossom, or grow flowers

daylight saving time: the time when clocks are set ahead one hour to give extra daylight in the evenings

Saint Patrick's Day: an Irish holiday. Some people wear the color green to celebrate.

spring: the season between winter and summer, when the air warms and flowers and plants begin to grow

vacation: time away from school or work

---

cambio de hora oficial: momento en que los relojes se adelantan para ganar una hora más de luz al final de la tarde

Día de San Patricio: fiesta irlandesa. Para celebrarlo, algunas personas se visten de verde.

florecer: salir las flores

primavera: la estación del año entre el invierno y el verano. En primavera, el aire se hace más caliente y las flores y las plantas empiezan a crecer.

vacaciones: periodo de descanso de las actividades de la escuela o del trabajo

For More Information/Más información

Books/Libros

How Tulips Grow/Cómo crecen los tulipanes. How Plants Grow/ Cómo crecen las plantas (series). Joanne Mattern (Gareth Stevens Publishing, 2006)

Spring/Primavera. Seasons of the Year/Las estaciones del año (series). JoAnn Early Macken (Gareth Stevens Publishing, 2006)

Web Sites/Páginas web

My First Garden/Mi primer jardín
www.urbanext.uiuc.edu/firstgarden
Learn how to grow a spring garden./Aprendan a sembrar un jardín de primavera.

Women's History Month/Mes de la Historia de la Mujer
www.history.com/minisites/womenhist
Get to know women who have changed history./Conozcan a mujeres que han cambiado la historia.

Publisher's note to educators and parents: Our editors have carefully reviewed these web sites to ensure that they are suitable for children. Many web sites change frequently, however, and we cannot guarantee that a site's future contents will continue to meet our high standards of quality and educational value. Be advised that children should be closely supervised whenever they access the Internet.

Nota de la editorial a los padres y educadores: Nuestros editores han revisado con cuidado las páginas web para asegurarse de que son apropiadas para niños. Sin embargo, muchas páginas web cambian con frecuencia, y no podemos garantizar que sus contenidos futuros sigan conservando nuestros elevados estándares de calidad y de interés educativo. Tengan en cuenta que los niños deben ser supervisados atentamente siempre que accedan a Internet.

Index/Índice

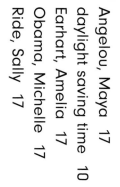

About the Author

Robyn Brode has been a teacher, a writer, and an editor in the book publishing field for many years. She earned a bachelor's degree in English literature from the University of California, Berkeley.

Información sobre la autora

Robyn Brode ha sido maestra, escritora y editora de libros durante muchos años. Obtuvo su licenciatura en literatura inglesa en la Universidad de California, Berkeley.